G000097453

A Touch of Christmas

A Touch of Christmas

Decorations for the Tree and Home

Pamela Allardice

Illustrated by Kate Mitchell

Angus&Robertson
An imprint of HarperCollins*Publishers*

CONTENTS

INTRODUCTION

Throughout the world, houses, churches and other meeting places are decorated with living greenery at Christmas. Many evergreens were worshipped in early times as seasonal talismans to protect against evil. To the pagans, these plants which refused to die symbolised the continuation of life, even when all the other trees were bare. At the feast of Saturnalia, Roman children exchanged boughs of green cypress or fir to herald the eventual return of spring, playfully slapping each other to ensure the good luck was passed on.

Older still is the traditional use of those plants which bear fruit in winter, especially mistletoe and holly. Our pagan forefathers believed the parasitic mistletoe plant held the life of the host plant during winter, saying that the berries contained the tree's precious seminal fluid. Druids revered mistletoe as sacred and would only cut it with a golden sickle.

As well as being a fertility symbol, mistletoe was thought to be a lucky charm against fire, earth and water, so sprigs were fastened above doorways as a symbol of hospitality, and enemies were encouraged to pledge truces by a mistletoe bough. This is one of the reasons behind the happy holiday custom of exchanging kisses under the mistletoe.

Much superstition surrounds holly. For instance, a holly hedge is thought to ward off witches. Holly is also strongly associated with Christ, mainly because of its thorny stem and blood-red berries, which have earned it the country name of "Christ's Crown". Holly is a male emblem and was thought to bring fertility to the household. Holly was also once used by romantically-minded young girls to divine a future lover. An old charm says to pick nine holly leaves at midnight on Christmas Eve, tie them in a handkerchief and put them under your pillow — you will then dream of your future partner. The earliest day when holly or mistletoe could safely be brought into the house (and only by a man, at that) was Christmas Eve. The holly branches were kept and burned under the following year's pudding as it boiled, which was supposedly a charm for luck.

With the advent of Christianity, religious significance was ascribed to all plants and herbs used in decoration. For instance, apples, which symbolised man's fall from grace, were baked with rosemary, to represent his redemption. The fragrant fir was deemed incense to honour God. The English, under the auspices of Queen Victoria, garlanded their homes inside and out with fir boughs; of particular importance in a Victorian home was the portrait of the bewhiskered family founder — this was always framed with a wreath of fir cones and greenery on Christmas Eve.

Bay leaves denoted great power, while cypress branches — though now often associated with graveyards — were used because their longevity connoted eternal life. Similarly yew trees, which can live for as long as a thousand years, were revered as a symbol of everlasting life.

Rosemary was strongly associated with Mary, the mother of Christ, having been said to have assumed its soft fragrance and hue when the Virgin flung her purple robe over a bush during the flight into Egypt. It was much prized as a token of remembrance at English Christmas feasts, where it was used to flavour the traditional boar's head.

In Australia, bowls of exotic poinsettias are popular Christmas decorations. Named after the man who introduced them to the United States (Dr Poinsett), the plants' bright yellow flowers and red leaves often feature on greeting cards. Mexicans exchange potted poinsettias as Christmas gifts and, according to local stories, the plant sprang from the earth where a child first knelt to pray. In South America, it is known as "Flower of the Holy Night" or "Star of Bethlehem".

Legends abound concerning the fir tree — for instance, a guardian cherub was said to have planted a fir cone on Adam's grave and the tree which eventually grew there provided the wood for Moses' miraculous staff. My favourite story about the Christmas tree tells of the time when the Christ Child was born, when all the trees in the forest travelled forth, their branches laden with their gifts of fruit, nuts and flowers. However, the little fir tree stood alone and asked the stars to come down and decorate its boughs. The baby Jesus clapped his hands with delight and declared fir trees should be decorated thus at Christmas for ever more to make children every-where happy.

Decorations used to trim early Christmas trees were quite simple — paper chains, gingerbread, strings of popcorn, gilded walnuts and rag bows. Roses, despite being summer-flowering plants, were associated with the traditional northern Christmas. Legend has it that a little shepherd girl of Bethlehem was sad for she had no gift to bring the Christ Child; suddenly an angel scattered beautiful white roses in her path which she gathered and laid in front of the manger — a pretty story which explains why paper, velvet and even china roses are often seen on Christmas trees.

The other main traditional tree decorations are the star, usually placed at the very top, and the bell. The star is, of course, associated with the story of the three Wise Men who "... when they saw the star ... rejoiced with exceeding great joy." (Matthew 2:10). In homes, stars often decorate a window or add attractiveness to Christmas biscuits, wrapping paper and greeting cards.

Bells are strongly associated with Christmas rejoicing. Church bells frequently peal out on Christmas Eve, and tradition credits St Nicholas with carrying a large bell in his hand. Strings of tiny silver or gold bells are often hung about the Christmas tree; as well, bells are found in outdoor wreaths or festive community street decorations.

Although Henry VIII's table was said to have been set with fir trees planted in pure gold tubs for Christmas, the English did not fully embrace the custom of decorating trees until Victoria's "dear Albert" set one up at Windsor Castle in 1841. Prince Albert's idea caught the public imagination and lavishly adorned trees became the centre-piece for all seasonal festivities.

Tree ornament production is now big business and simple made-it-myself decorations appear to be a ghost of Christmas past; however, the spirit of tree-decorating lives on in the story of the humble tinsel. This tells of a woman who cut a fir tree for her children in a determined effort to provide them with a little Christmas cheer; she could not, however, afford decorations or candles. During the night, spiders wove pretty webs through the branches and God, admiring the woman's sweet unselfishness, turned them to silver.

DECORATIONS FOR
the Home

CHRISTMAS WREATH

The custom of hanging Christmas wreaths on the front door originated in Scandinavia, as the circular shape was a witch repellent. This practice was also adopted in Ireland, where a popular door decoration was a cross made of holly.

Simple evergreen wreaths can be made at home or bought from florists. Canes pruned from grape vines can easily be woven together to form the base for a wreath, as can willow, wisteria or birch stems. They look so attractive that they need little decoration. Alternatively, buy a stout wire and oasis ring, or a straw wreath, from a craft supplies shop. Pad it with florist's moss or raffia to disguise the base. Don't bother trying to make one from coat-hangers — they tend to buckle. Holly is the traditional evergreen for a wreath, but any evergreen can be used. Ivy, box and yew can all be cut in 30–45 cm (12–18 in) lengths and bound thickly around the frame before being secured with a glossy red ribbon. To keep evergreens fresh, leave them in water for as long as possible before making your wreath.

For a fancier wreath, you might like to tuck in tiny bundles of spices, flowers, nuts or grasses, selecting from the suggestions below.

- ❖ *everlasting dried flowers*
- ❖ *pine cones and berries*
- ❖ *tiny pomegranates dusted with clear glitter, or gilded*
- ❖ *small silver or gold balls*
- ❖ *vanilla pods, cinnamon sticks, star anise*
- ❖ *gilded bay leaves, lapped one over the other*
- ❖ *poppy seed cases, rosemary sprigs, chestnuts and other unshelled nuts, nutmegs, all sprayed with clear lacquer or gold paint*

Start at one side and work around. In this way, all the decoration will travel in the same direction, overlapping to conceal the stems. Dust with gold leaf and attach with gold braid or gauzy golden ribbon to make the wreath look really festive and glittering for Christmas.

STARLIGHT CANDLES

Set two slim, elegant red candles in a styrofoam base or florist's mount. Stick gummed gold and silver stars, back to back, at random along lengths of very fine but quite firm fuse wire. Garland the candles with a loose "cloud" of starred wire and light them — they will look as though they are floating among the stars.

A TOUCH OF CHRISTMAS

4

WINDOW DECORATIONS

Watch your windows come alive with any of the following ideas.

★ Create a stained glass window. Cut shapes out of bright green, yellow, red and blue cellophane and tape firmly to the window in a design.

★ Use a single candle or a group, decorated with some greenery and fir cones, on a windowsill to show a friendly light to passers-by.

A TOUCH OF CHRISTMAS

WINDOW MOBILE

Collect together a piece of cane as long as the width of the window; bright blue, red or dark green double-sided card; white or silver paint and a brush; and a needle and thread. Cut out different sized shapes from the card, approx-imately 2.5–7.5 cm (1–3 in) wide. Squares and circles make an effective contrast. Punch a small hole at the top of each shape, then decorate each side with a snowflake design using the white paint. Hang shapes from the piece of cane, varying the length of the threads so they fall in a pretty pattern. Attach threads to both ends of the cane and use these to hang the mobile from the top of the window mounting.

IVY-COVERED CANDLESTICKS

Like holly, ivy is thought to possess powerful medicinal properties. For example, an ivy leaf in either shoe protects the wearer from corns. Ivy is also thought to be a romantic plant: an old Twelfth Night love charm was for a girl to hold a piece of ivy to her heart and recite:

> "Ivy, ivy, I love you,
> In my bosom I put you,
> The first young man who speaks to me,
> My true husband shall he be."

Cut long trailing strands of ivy and let them fall elegantly from a basket filled with a mixture of other evergreens. A pair of candlesticks, set in old-fashioned holders with strands of ivy pinned to twine around them, are a sentimental favourite for the sideboard. A very traditional gift is to pot up a holly seedling and set ivy all around its base.

Luminarias

Luminarias are sand-weighted paper bags with lighted candles inside them. They are most effective when placed close together in large numbers, so allow time to make quite a few. For each luminaria, you will need a medium-sized, square-based brown paper bag, one cup of sand and a squat candle. Fold the top of the bag down until the top is only 7.5–12 cm (3–5 in) high. Pour the sand into the bag, anchor the candle firmly in the centre and light it. The candles will burn down safely and there is little danger of fire — but keep small children away, nonetheless.

VICTORIAN KISSING-BALL

These were very popular in fine homes in the latter part of the nineteenth century. Men were at liberty to claim a kiss from any girl "casually" standing beneath the ball, plucking a mistletoe berry for each forfeit. When all the berries were gone, the kissing was supposed to stop.

To make a kissing-ball, tie two hoops of wire or wood together to make a globe shape. Decorate it lavishly, twining it with ribbons, tinsel and evergreens such as ivy, then hang a cluster of mistletoe in the centre. Fruits and nuts may be threaded on bright streamers and dangled from it. For the ambitious, wire a miniature crib scene in the centre to represent the Nativity. Hang the kissing-ball in the centre of your living or dining room, or in the main entrance to the house.

THE NATIVITY SCENE

The Christmas crib was first popularised by St Francis of Assisi, who set up a simple manger scene at the little town of Greccio in Italy in 1224. It included a real manger and straw, a live ox and an ass, and local villagers who took the parts of Mary, Joseph and the shepherds. The ceremony proved so popular it was repeated each year.

To make your nativity scene, you will need a large, firm cardboard box with one side cut out, plus twigs, leaves and straw or dried grass. Glue the larger twigs and leaves over and around the box, inside and out, to make the stable. Scatter smaller pieces of dried grass or snipped lengths of straw inside the base of the box for a floor. Straw may also be placed lengthwise across the top of the box to create an impression of a roof; alternatively, glue fir cone pieces in an overlapping pattern as tiles.

Dolls can be used for the Holy Family and Three Kings. However, children could try making the figures themselves from playdough, modelling wax or plasticine. To dress the figures, select scraps from the family's rag-bag — flannel, cotton or fine felt for Joseph and Mary, a scrap of white muslin for the baby Jesus, and any glamorous pieces of satin or brocade for the Wise Men. Hats and crowns may be fashioned from cardboard or from cloth sprayed with fabric stiffener. As a finishing touch, wire a big gold paper star to "hang" in the sky above the stable roof. If the scene is quite large, you may have room to wire one or two paper angels to the stable roof as well.

ADVENT RING

The Advent Ring is a symbolic and beautiful focus for a room, especially as a dining table centrepiece, and a means of reminding people of the season. Four candle holders are secured around a large evergreen wreath with a large candle holder wired in the centre. A red candle is placed in each holder on each Advent Sunday, with the largest one going into place on Christmas Day, when they are all lit.

Make an Advent ring using a purchased cane or wicker circular base. Wind lengths of evergreen around the frame — traditionally, yew and ivy are used. Secure two straight wire or rope supporters diagonally across the ring, making an X-shape in the centre, and bind these with evergreen too. Secure four small, round, red candles around the circle and one large one in the central cross-piece. Place the ring in the centre of the festive table.

ADVENT CALENDAR

The Germans are thought to have initiated the custom of distributing Advent calendars to children. These designs have changed very little and are still usually silver-frosted landscapes with 25 hinged openings which are numbered with the date when they may be opened, leading up to Christmas. Each little door yields a secret picture or message, or perhaps a small present.

To make your own Advent calendar, take a piece of heavy drawing paper or light card and sketch your design, for example a house, a forest scene, even an abstract "stained glass" type of design. Mark where you wish to place the 25 windows on your design. Colour or paint the design and, then, placing it on a piece of thick card or a self-healing cutting mat or board, use a razor, Stanley knife or thin-bladed knife to carefully cut around three sides of each window.

Cut a second sheet of paper or card the same size as your first — by tracing just inside the lines where the windows will be, mark the outline where your pictures or messages will go. Use your imagination here — you can draw pictures of animals, presents or stockings, favourite cartoons or riddles, or symbols such as the moon and stars. You might also like to try pasting family photos or pictures from magazines — or even telling a story or poem, line by line. Spread craft glue carefully on the back of your design sheet, thinly around the edges of the windows, then press firmly over the second sheet.

CHILDREN'S TREES

Helping decorate the house for Christmas is a perfect project for children. The next time your children are bewailing their boredom during school holidays, try sitting them down to a Christmas project of their own. They'll stay occupied for hours.

A sweet tree — collect an armful of largish fallen twigs, spread them out on newspaper (preferably in the back garden) and spray or paint with silver, white or gold paint. Secure the twigs in small pots packed with earth, sand or modelling clay and then hang wrapped sweets from the branches.

A tree for the birds — household decorations and festivities should not be confined to the indoors. In Scandinavian countries, a sheaf of grain is attached to a pole and placed outside in the snow-covered yard as a Christmas gift for the birds. Whether for robins in a northern hemisphere or rosellas in the south, children can help make and hang feeders in a special "tree for the birds" and so help deck the garden with bright, darting colour and song in time for Christmas.

A beach tree — find a large piece of driftwood and secure different twigs or wire to it as "branches" before arranging the child's collection of beach treasures. Pretty pebbles or shells can be given a coat of clear varnish or painted with humorous faces or small pictures before being heaped around the base of the "tree".

A little girl's fairy tree — decorate a small white or silver artificial tree with rosebuds and gauzy butterflies. Hair slides provide a marvellous selection of ornaments to choose from. Cover the base with silver or pink cord and tassels.

GIANT POMPOM

This looks particularly striking when placed by the front door or at the turn of a staircase. Collect together a 1.5 m (5 ft) length of cane, narrow multi-coloured ribbons, holly and/or mistletoe or flowers (real or artificial) and fine chicken wire. Bunch wire into a large thick ball and wedge it securely to one end of the cane; tape or wire the cane to the base of the ball to make quite sure it will not move. Decorate cane by winding ribbons round and round it. Decorate wire ball with holly and/or mistletoe, twists of tissue paper and clusters of flowers, berries or gilded leaves — whatever takes your fancy. As a finishing touch, tuck bunches of ribbons into the ball so they cascade out over the cane.

CHRISTMAS CENTREPIECES

A stylish and dramatic centrepiece which is a little bit different can be made from skeleton leaves — magnolia leaves are very suitable. Soak the leaves for 48 hours in a mixture of 1 tablespoon household bleach to 500 ml (18 oz) warm water. The leaves' flesh can then be easily stripped from the leaves and the delicate "skeletons" dried thoroughly before being sprayed with red, gold or silver paint. Decorate with clusters of glass baubles in a contrasting colour and shake glitter over the whole arrangement for a sparkling, fairy tale effect.

PEARLY APPLE SASH

A different, fresh touch for a door or wall decoration — pierce bright green apples with pearl-headed pins and cloves in decorative patterns. Tie them together from their stems with fine silver string or cord and gather loosely, swag-style, with a bow of green and silver striped ribbon.

FROSTED FRUITS

No old-fashioned Christmas would really be complete without a dish on the sideboard piled high with pretty frosted fruits. Use small fruits, such as grapes, plums, Christmas apples, peaches or slices of orange or grapefruit. Wash fruit and dry it thoroughly. Lightly whisk 1–2 egg whites and coat each piece of fruit thoroughly using a fine paint brush. Dust with caster sugar and set aside to dry before heaping high on a decorative dish.

CHRISTMAS PENNANTS

A very simple project for even quite small children is to create all sorts of brightly coloured pennants to hang on walls or doors. Simply cut long strips of paper — about 1 metre long and 15 cm wide (3 feet x 6 inches) — and decorate them. Children can either cut letters out for a message, like "Merry Christmas" from foil, or make cottonwool faces of snowmen and Santa Claus, and paste them to the pennants.

DECORATING WITH CHRISTMAS CARDS

This is probably the easiest as well as the most universally cheerful way of decorating the house. Christmas cards make charming displays on the mantelpiece or tucked in with books and ornaments on shelves. They can also make a warm welcome if you have a glass door — simply tape cards to the glass at decorative angles.

Fir Cone Swags

Collect fir or pine tree cones and store them until it is time
to make Christmas decorations. Many other trees produce
beautifully-shaped nuts which also add an old-fashioned and
traditional touch to a Christmas tree. Either paint
individual nuts and cones gold or silver and hang them
from the tree, or wrap nuts in silver foil and glue them back
in their natural cases. To make an attractive swag for the
front door, wire or tie together cones and nuts of various
shapes and sizes, using a length of twisted heavy wire,
hessian or a hank of coloured wools as a base. Tie lengths of
brightly coloured ribbons to the swag and decorate with
small bells or greenery. If the swag is a large one, use it as a
wall decoration and staple Christmas cards to it.

Paper Chains

Buy the flat packets of coloured crepe paper and experiment with different colour combinations — try bright pink, lemon, gold, plum, turquoise and lavender — to add sparkle and fun to the home. Unfold the paper once and cut lengthwise strips about 4 cm wide by 15 cm long (1½ in x 6 in). Make a loop from one strip and secure with a dot of glue; thread through a strip in a contrasting colour and glue that, and so on. Smaller, thinner lengths of paper chain may be used to decorate the tree. Choose Christmas wrapping paper for this, rather than crepe paper, as it is a little firmer to work with.

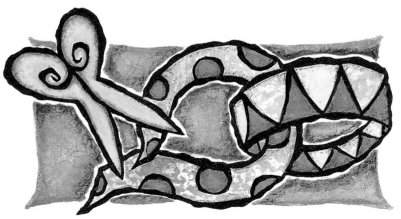

Fringed Streamers

Take three packs of different coloured crepe paper, fold out lengthwise and cut long strips from each colour, about 8 cm (3 in) wide. Holding strips on top of each other, feed evenly through a sewing machine, stitching a long seam down the middle. Snip a fine fringe to the centre seam from both sides of the streamer. Tease out ends and hang up. (Tip: twisting this streamer as it is looped over the tree or across a wall will show off the colours.)

Starlight Chains

Cut long strips of dark blue tissue paper. Fold to and fro at approximately 5 cm (2 in) intervals. Using small sharp scissors, cut out a simple five-pointed star, then pull out paper to form a chain. Spray lightly with adhesive and scatter with silver glitter. These chains look quite transparent and magical; however, tissue is very fragile, so it is only for the patient.

DECORATIVE CHAINS

Different ideas for decking walls, ceiling, bannisters and curtain rods, as well as the tree ...

Pierce holes in different-sized and shaped pieces of pasta; space along string by knotting; and paint with glossy enamel.

Alternate different coloured paper chop ruffles, separated with lengths of coloured drinking straws.

Staple two cupcake papers one inside the other. Staple another pair back to back. Make clusters of large and small papers and decorate. Thread on glittery cord in alternating sizes.

Holiday Tablecloth

Dress up a bright red or green cloth by sewing little golden or silver bells to the hem. Everyone will enjoy the occasional jingles at the table as they brush against the cloth.

Or, you could easily make a bright holiday runner to contrast with your usual tablecloth: a red gingham one, for instance. Edge the runner with gold rick-rack and decorate it with Christmas motifs. A "wrapped" Christmas table is easy to achieve by taking two strips of extra-wide satin ribbon and running them across the table to resemble a gift. Tie a large flat bow in one corner.

ORNAMENTS FOR
the Tree

Fragrant Wax Ornaments

Melt some candle wax or beeswax and stir in a few drops of aromatic essential oil — pine, rosemary and juniper are all suitable. Pour into lightly greased decorative moulds, embedding a loop of gold thread in the top before they harden (unless mould has a "loop" fixture already). Unmould and hang on the tree. (Tip: many chocolate-making kits have imaginative moulds, such as boots, roses, kittens, birds and little houses.)

Bead Loops

A cinch for even small children to make. Collect together needle, thread or fine nylon and plenty of small bright beads or old buttons. Cut 15 cm (6 in) lengths of thread or nylon, tie a knot in one end and string with the beads or buttons. Bring ends together and tie securely, tucking loose ends of threads back into beads; then hang loops from the tips of tree branches.

SCENTED TREE SACHETS

Sachets filled with herbs and spices look pretty hanging on the tree, and make everything smell fresh and airy.

Cut out two sides (round, heart or diamond-shaped) from a pretty piece of fabric, such as bright gingham. Bits of antique brocade or scraps of shot silk can be made up into exquisite sachets. Pieces of lace lined with white or pastel tulle also look very pretty. Sew up three of the edges of the sachet, turn, and pad with light stuffing (quilt batting is ideal). Place a spoonful of potpourri inside the padding and sew that up. Use ribbon or silken cord to make a loop to hang the sachet by. This blend is spicy and long-lasting:

30g (1 oz) rosemary, crushed
15g (¼ oz) cinnamon sticks, crushed
30g (1 oz) cedar shavings
30g (1 oz) whole cloves
1 tbspn orris root powder
few drops oil of cedar or patchouli

SILVERY CIRCLES

Even very small children have plenty of fun making these. If little fingers mean the foil gets all wrinkled instead of being smooth, so much the better, because this means the circles sparkle in the light.

Take the cardboard centre left over from a roll of paper towels and slice it up like a jam roll about 0.5 to 1.25 cm (¼ to ½ in), depending on the firmness of the card. Cut silver foil into even strips and wrap each circle so no cardboard shows. Hang the silvery circles from the tree on lengths of silver ribbon or thread.

PRETTY POMANDERS

Citrus fruits and apples spiked with cloves can be piled into china bowls or cured in a bowl of spice mixture and tied to the tree with beautiful ribbons. You will need:

- ❖ *small, firm, thin-skinned fruits, such as apples, crabapples, lemons, limes or oranges*

- ❖ *whole cloves, with strong stems and large heads*

- ❖ *a thin metal knitting needle or bodkin*

- ❖ *spice mixture — 115 g (4 oz) ground cinnamon; 50 g (2 oz) ground nutmeg; 50 g (2 oz) ground ginger; 25 g (1 oz) allspice; 50 g (2 oz) orris root powder*

- ❖ *narrow ribbon*

Gently knead fruit to soften skin, then punch small holes all over it with needle or bodkin, leaving two narrow strips cross-wise around the fruit to act as a groove to hold the ribbon. Stick cloves into holes. Roll fruit in spice mixture and pat it in well with your fingers so it is thoroughly coated. Wrap fruit in tissue paper and leave it in a dark, airy place for 2 to three weeks or until hard and quite dry. Tie ribbon around unstudded strips and secure top with a bow. Add a loop in a contrasting ribbon to hang pomander by. Alternatively, tie fruit into small bags of brightly coloured net or tulle and thread a ribbon through the top of that.

Tree Angels

Collect together a paper towel tube; medium-weight card-board; coloured felt; small, medium and large sequins; glue; pinking shears; ping-pong ball; wire and tinsel.

Cut tube to a 7.5 cm (3 in) length. Cut skirt and wing shapes from cardboard. Roll cardboard "skirt" tightly around top of tube, allowing it to flare out at bottom edge; overlap edges and glue to secure. Cut felt scraps with pinking shears and glue to base in a decorative pattern — lengthwise strips are easiest. Decorate with sequins. Paste sequins onto wings, leaving a strip down the centre back where they may be glued to the back of the angel. Paint a face on the ping-pong ball and glue to top of tube. Make a tiny halo by twisting wire into a ring and twining with tinsel; secure with an extra length of wire concealed down the angel's back between the wings.

Gingerbread Tree Decorations

Decorate these pretty biscuits with different coloured icing, then thread them on white ribbons or natural raffia before tying them to the tree.

4 tablespoons butter
2 cups brown sugar
2 eggs, well beaten
2 tablespoons milk
4 tablespoons golden syrup
2 teaspoons bicarbonate of soda
½ teaspoon almond essence
4 cups plain flour
2 teaspoons ground cinnamon
3 teaspoons ground ginger
1 teaspoon allspice
1 teaspoon cream of tartar

Cream butter and sugar; add eggs and beat until mixture thickens. Combine milk, golden syrup, bicarbonate of soda and almond essence and add to egg mixture. Sift flour, cinnamon, ginger, allspice and cream of tartar together and stir into mixture, mixing very well. Shape dough into a rectangle and roll out on well-floured board to 1 cm (½ in) thick.

Using decorative cutters — hearts, stars and crescent moons all look good — cut out shapes and, with a metal or wooden skewer, make a hole at the top of each for threading. Place on baking sheets lined with greaseproof paper and cook for 20 to 30 minutes in 200° C (400° F) oven. Do not allow them to brown. Let cookies cool on racks then decorate with spread or piped design in coloured icing.

CONFETTI BALLS

Cut a piece of stiff cardboard about 5 cm x 7 cm (2 in x 3 in), and wind multicoloured wool thickly over it lengthwise. Securing ends with fingers, sew around centre firmly, without touching card. Slip wound wool off card and twist extra threads tightly around stitched centre and secure. Slit ends of wool and fluff out so they form a soft, colourful tassel-like ball. Use a longer piece of the wool, or nylon thread, to make a loop to hang from the tree.

CHRISTMAS ROSES

Beautiful ornamental flowers can be made from velvet, silk — even feathers. The simplest way to make sensational roses, either for display or to twist through the tree's branches, is to use crepe paper. The flowers need not be realistic — in fact, the more fantastic they are, the better. Use silver foil for the stems and tiny pearl beads or rhinestone chips for the stamens to add a glamorous touch.

First, make the centre of the flower by folding a piece of
satin or paper over some wadding and securing tightly.
Wire the flower's stamens in place, tucking ends under
flower's centre and out of sight. Attach short piece of wire
to underside of flower centre to act as a base for the stem.
Cut petals out of crepe paper, using a heart-shaped pattern,
and wrap them around the flower centre, furling tightly at
first and then blousing the outer petals outwards,
stretching the rim of the paper with your thumbs. Secure
base of flower petals with green florist's tape and then wrap
wired stem thickly with either fine felt, satin or foil.

A TOUCH OF CHRISTMAS

CORNUCOPIAS

Give your tree a Victorian air with cornucopias. Collect together small pointed ice cream cones or purchased cardboard cones; rubber bands; some netting or tulle; ribbon and plenty of small sweets, marzipan fruits or party favours. Cut the net into squares large enough to wrap each cone completely, leaving enough material to form a ruffle at the top. Fill each cone with sweets, then wrap with the netting and secure with rubber band and ribbon bow, fanning out the ends attractively. Hang from tree with a ribbon loop.

MACARONI TREE ORNAMENTS

Pasta comes in all sorts of odd shapes and sizes. Buy a wide variety and use food colouring to dye them all sorts of different shades. Let the children thread them on string and they will become cherished personal tree decorations. Older children can make more elaborate macaroni ornaments. Dip the pieces rapidly in hot water to soften and then shape them; they could experiment with making goblins and fairies, using elbow macaroni for arms and legs. Let the macaroni ornaments dry, then paint them with bright nail polish or gloss enamel.

CHRISTMAS HEARTS

Collect together scraps of red felt, or satin; small shiny beads or sequins; narrow ribbon; and polyester fibre wadding. Trace and cut out front and back for heart on red felt or satin for each ornament. With right sides together, pin heart front to back and stitch in narrow seam, leaving a small opening. Clip curves and turn. Stuff with wadding and, turning edges inwards, stitch opening closed. Decorate with clusters of red beads or sequins. Make loop from ribbon and stitch to the top of the heart as a hanger.

SPARKLY STARS

Wire four plastic cocktail picks together in the centre to form a star shape. Wind thread around and around shape, twisting around each pick to secure, to form a 'web'. Dip the whole star first in glue, then in glitter. Let dry, then attach to tree using silver ribbon.

SUGAR PLUMS

500 g (1 lb) prunes, stones removed
500 g (1 lb) icing sugar
tulle, cut into squares
fine ribbon

Steam prunes for 40 to 50 minutes, or until they have plumped up well. Drain. Scatter icing sugar thickly on a plate and roll each prune two or three times. Cover with plastic cling wrap, set aside and allow to cool. Wrap each "sugar plum" in a tulle square, tie with ribbon and hang from the tree.

Paper Birds

In Sweden, a decorative paper bird is traditionally suspended over the dining table to bring peace to the household in the coming year. Smaller ones can be made in different pastel colours and hung on the Christmas tree.

Collect together cardboard and tissue paper. Cut the body of a bird from the cardboard. Make two small slits, one near the "tail" about 1.5 mm (⅟₁₆ in) long and one a little wider in the centre where the wings will go. Cut strips of tissue approximately 10 cm x 22 cm (4 in x 9 in) and fold, to and fro, in 1.5 cm (½ in) pleats. Staple or stitch in the centre, then work through slits and secure with tiny patches of sticky tape. Fan out pleats of tail and wings, then run a loop through the top of the bird's body to hang it by.

CORKSCREWS

Cut a circle of light card or firm paper and decorate with glitter. Starting from the outside, cut a continuous even line towards the centre, about 0.5 cm (¼ in) wide. Punch a hole in the centre and hang ornament by a hook made from fine wire, pulling the curled strip out gently.

MEXICAN-STYLE FOIL ORNAMENTS

Bright, shiny tinplate ornaments are sold in Mexico as tourist mementos. To make similar decorations, buy heavy silver foil (from craft or home decorator shops). Lay the foil down flat and trace out patterns, using different shaped cookie cutters. Cut out shapes, punch a hole in the top and then place face-down on top of several thicknesses of paper. Emboss with a pattern — simple dots and lines look the best — by pressing firmly into the back of the foil with a blunted knitting needle or bodkin. Hang using a length of fine gold or silver thread.

RAFFLE PRIZE ORNAMENTS

If you have a large enough tree, decorate it with small presents, each wrapped and numbered. These could contain sweets, or small gifts, like handkerchiefs or a pack of cards — that way it doesn't really matter who wins what. Write the numbers from the presents on small pieces of paper, fold them up tightly, and mix them up in a hat or basket. Everyone then picks a number and claims a prize from the tree. This is particularly good fun for a children's Christmas party.

Gilded Walnuts

Collect together walnut half-shells; rubber gloves; metallic gold-coloured enamel paint; newspaper; old cake racks; darning needle and gilt thread. Pour paint into large plastic or foil container. Put on gloves and spread out newspaper for drying shells. Dip shells into enamel, one at a time, then place them face down on old cake racks over newspaper to dry. Retouch any smudged parts with a fine-tipped paintbrush. When shells are dry, thread needle with gold thread and pierce shells near top to string them. (Tip: to stop shells clustering together, thread beads in between.)

 # Lace Stars

Children love cutting up paper doilies to make these pretty ornaments for the tree. Simply fold each doily into eight, then cut out a triangular wedge from the bottom. Unfold to reveal star. Push loop of silver thread through doily to hang on tree.

DECORATED EGGS

Pierce the pointed end of an egg with a fine needle, then make a slightly larger hole in the flatter end. Let white and yolk run out, rinse shell carefully and dry. Take a length of fine thread, tie a knot in one end and thread through fine hole and up through larger one. Decorate the shell with tiny beads, glitter, paint, lace or bright nail varnish. Use foil or green felt holly leaves to disguise hole in top of egg.

THE TREE FAIRY

A Barbie doll is probably the most appropriate, being light enough to secure to the tree.

First make a bodice for the doll by wrapping a strip of fabric around her chest, tucking under rough edges and gluing to secure. Make a skirt by cutting several stiff net circles, then cutting a hole in the centre and sliding the doll through. Secure skirt at waist with tinsel or ribbon and let your child decorate it. Make a magic wand by wrapping a toothpick with foil; decorate with glitter and a coloured paper star.

A TOUCH OF CHRISTMAS

An Angus & Robertson Publication

Angus&Robertson, an imprint of
HarperCollins *Publishers*
25 Ryde Road, Pymble, Sydney NSW 2073, Australia
31 View Road, Glenfield, Auckland 10, New Zealand
77–85 Fulham Palace Road London W6 8JB, United Kingdom
10 East 53rd Street, New York NY 10022, USA

First published in Australia in 1994

Copyright © Pamela Allardice 1994
Illustrations © Kate Mitchell 1994

This book is copyright.
Apart from any fair dealing for the purposes of private study, research,
criticism or review, as permitted under the Copyright Act, no part may
be reproduced by any process without written permission. Inquiries
should be addressed to the publishers.

National Library of Australia
Cataloguing-in-Publication data:
Allardice, Pamela, 1958-.
A touch of Christmas: decorations for the tree and home.
ISBN 0 207 18598 0
1. Christmas decorations. 2. Handicraft. I. Title. II Title: Decorations
for the tree and home.
745.59412

Designed by Robyn Latimer

Printed in Australia by Griffin Press, Adelaide

98 97 96 95 94
9 8 7 6 5 4 3 2 1